BUDGET MEALS

Edited by Jane Solmson

WEATHERVANE BOOKS
New York

Copyright © MCMLXXX by Ottenheimer Publishers, Inc.
All rights reserved.
Library of Congress Catalog Card Number: 80-50644

This edition is published by Weathervane Books,
 distributed by Crown Publishers, Inc.
a b c d e f g h

Published under arrangement with Ottenheimer Publishers, Inc.
Printed in the United States of America

CONTENTS

SALADS

Marinated Cucumber and Pepper Salad

2 large cucumbers, sliced thin

Season cucumbers with salt; let stand in colander to drain. Press out gently. Pat dry with towel.

5 green peppers
Salt
Pepper
2 tablespoons lemon juice
Salad oil

Mix cucumbers and peppers.

Toss with pepper, lemon juice, and a little oil. Let marinate 2 hours.

2 hard-boiled eggs

Garnish with eggs.

Yield: 8 servings.

Macaroni Salad

Excellent as an accompaniment to any broiled meat.

2 cups shell or ring macaroni

Cook macaroni in boiling salted water; drain well.

2 tablespoons butter
1 cup cubed cheddar cheese
1 cup sliced gherkins
½ cup very finely chopped onion
2 cups cooked peas

Add butter; toss lightly.
Add cheese, gherkins, onion, and peas.

½ cup mayonnaise

Stir in mayonnaise; blend carefully, making sure macaroni is well mixed with mayonnaise.

Seasoning

Check seasoning.

Set aside to chill.

Lettuce

Serve individually in lettuce leaves or on bed of shredded lettuce.

Yield: 6 servings.

5

Potato Salad

½ cup mayonnaise
2 tablespoons prepared
  mustard

2 tablespoons minced onion
¼ cup (generous) pickle
  relish

2 pounds potatoes (cooked,
  peeled, diced—1 quart)
½ cup thinly sliced celery
½ of a small green or red
  pepper, seeded, chopped
  fine
Salt and pepper to taste

Paprika for garnish

In bowl gradually whisk mayonnaise into mustard.

Stir in onion and relish.

Add potatoes, celery, green pepper, and salt and pepper;
  toss well.

Chill several hours or overnight to allow flavors to blend.

Garnish with paprika.

Yield: 6 servings.

Potato Salad

Hot Slaw

1 medium cabbage,
  shredded

¼ cup chopped onion
½ cup sour cream
½ cup mayonnaise
1 teaspoon prepared
  mustard
1 teaspoon lemon juice
Pinch of sugar
Salt to taste

Place cabbage in small amount of boiling salted water;
  cover.
Cook rapidly until tender-crisp (3 to 5 minutes, depending
  on how finely shredded); drain.

Add onion, sour cream, mayonnaise, mustard, and lemon
  juice to cabbage.

Blend in sugar and salt.

Stir over low heat until heated through.

Yield: 6 to 8 servings.

Sauerkraut Salad

1 large can (No. 2½)
    sauerkraut

Rinse sauerkraut; drain 15 minutes.

1 large green pepper,
    chopped fine
1 large onion, chopped fine
2 carrots (grated) or 4 table-
    spoons diced pimiento

Add pepper, onion, and carrots; mix thoroughly.

½ cup water
½ cup vinegar
1 cup sugar
½ teaspoon salt

Boil water, vinegar, sugar, and salt 1 minute; let cool.
Pour over kraut mixture; let set.
The longer it sets the better it is.

Will keep indefinitely if refrigerated.

Yield: 10 servings.

Turkey and Kidney–Bean Salad

1 cup leftover turkey pieces
1¼ cups cooked or canned
    kidney beans, drained
⅓ cup chopped sweet
    pickle
⅔ cup coarsely chopped
    celery
1 tablespoon finely chopped
    onion
2 hard-cooked eggs, diced
1 teaspoon salt
3 tablespoons mayonnaise
1 teaspoon pickle liquid
1 teaspoon prepared
    mustard

Combine all ingredients; toss lightly.

Chill at least 1 hour to blend flavors.

Yield: about 6 servings.

Spinach with Peanuts

1 pound fresh spinach,
    washed, stemmed

Steam spinach in small amount boiling water 2 to 3
    minutes.
Drain at once; pat dry.
Cut into fine strips.

¼ cup (or more) peanuts

Crush half the peanuts with rolling pin or mince with
    cleaver.

1 tablespoon vegetable oil
1 tablespoon soy sauce
Salt and pepper

Heat oil in wok or skillet.
Add peanuts, spinach, soy sauce, and salt and pepper to
    taste.
Stir-fry 1 to 2 minutes.
Serve garnished with remaining peanuts.

Yield: 4 servings.

Vegetable-Bean Salad

1-pound can kidney beans
1-pound can green beans
1-pound can wax beans
1-pound can chick peas
½ of 6-ounce can pitted
   olives
¼ pound fresh mushrooms,
   sliced, or 1 small can
1 medium onion, diced
¼ cup chopped green
   pepper
½ cup chopped celery

¼ cup vegetable oil
½ cup white vinegar
1 teaspoon oregano
1 teaspoon sweet basil
1 tablespoon sugar

Drain beans, olives, and mushrooms (if canned).
Combine with other vegetables.

Mix together remaining ingredients; pour over beans and
   vegetables.

Refrigerate several hours before serving.

Yield: about 10 servings.

Jellied Vegetable Salad

3-ounce package lemon-
   flavored gelatin
1 teaspoon unflavored
   gelatin
1 cup boiling water
1 cup cold water
1 teaspoon finely chopped
   onion
½ teaspoon salt

¼ cup chopped green
   pepper
¼ cup shredded carrots
¼ cup diced celery
¼ cup thinly sliced radishes

Several lettuce leaves

Combine gelatins.
Dissolve in boiling water.

Add cold water, onion, and salt.
Chill in refrigerator until mixture begins to thicken.

Gently stir in green pepper, carrots, celery, and radishes.
Pour into 1-quart mold or 6 individual molds.
Chill until set.

Unmold by dipping mold in pan of warm water for a few
   seconds.

Serve on lettuce.

Yield: 6 servings.

Turkey or Chicken Salad

3 cups cooked, diced turkey
or chicken
1 cup diced celery
½ teaspoon salt, or as
desired
⅛ teaspoon pepper
1 tablespoon minced onion
1 tablespoon lemon juice
(optional)
½ cup mayonnaise or salad
dressing or ⅓ cup French
dressing

Mix all ingredients gently.
Chill before serving.

Yield: 6 servings.

Turkey or Chicken Fruit Salad

Omit 1 cup turkey or chicken.
Add 1 cup seedless grapes or pineapple chunks.

Marinated Bean Sprouts

An excellent salad to serve with meat or fish, this has a unique flavor. Try it for guests who like to sample something a little unusual.

1 pound fresh bean sprouts

Place bean sprouts in colander; blanch.
Immediately rinse with cold water; drain well.

Marinade
3 tablespoons chopped
scallion (use green and
white parts)
2 tablespoons sesame-seed
oil
2 tablespoons soy sauce
1 tablespoon vodka
1 tablespoon vinegar

Combine remaining ingredients in large bowl.

Place bean sprouts in mixture.
Marinate at room temperature 1 hour.

Refrigerate at least 3 hours before serving.
Yield: 4 servings.

SOUPS

White Bean Soup

1 pound dried navy beans
3 quarts water

Cover beans with water in large pot or soup kettle; soak overnight.

Smoked ham bone or ham hock

Rinse beans well; return to pot with ham bone and 3 quarts water.
Simmer uncovered 2 hours.

2 tablespoons chopped parsley
1 cup finely chopped onions
1 clove garlic, minced
2 cups finely chopped celery with green tops
1½ teaspoons salt
½ teaspoon pepper

Add parsley, onions, garlic, celery, salt, and pepper.
Simmer uncovered 1 hour or until vegetables are tender.

Remove ham bone; dice meat.
Add meat to soup.

Serve hot.

Yield: 8 servings.

Beet Soup

2 large raw beets

Wash 2 large beets.
Cook in salted water until tender. Drain, peel, and cube them.

2 tablespoons butter
1 tablespoon flour
4 cups meat broth
2 teaspoons sugar
1 tablespoon vinegar
½ teaspoon salt

Melt butter in 2-quart pot.
Add flour; stir until very smooth.
Add hot meat broth; stir mixture until it comes to boil.
Add sugar, cubed beets, vinegar, and salt.
Cook mixture over low heat about 2 hours.

1 small raw beet
Sour cream for garnish (optional)

Grate small beet. Sprinkle into soup before serving.
Top with spoonful of whipped sour cream.

Yield: 6 servings.

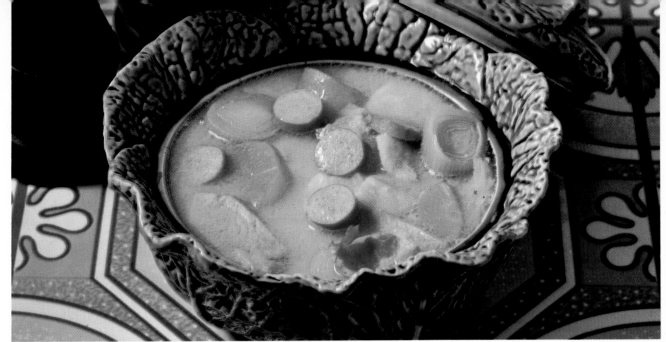

Cabbage Soup

Cabbage Soup

1 small green cabbage (2 cups shredded)	Slice and wash green cabbage. Put into pan of boiling salted water. Cook 5 minutes. Drain; rinse under cold water.
2 slices fat bacon	Meanwhile, chop bacon; heat over gentle heat until fat runs.
1 large onion, chopped **2 small leeks, white part only, sliced** **2 carrots, sliced**	Add onion, leeks, carrots, and potato.
1 potato, sliced **1 tablespoon flour** **4 cups brown stock (or water and cubes—ham stock can be used, if not too salty)**	Stir over heat a few minutes. Sprinkle in flour. Blend well before adding stock.
2 tablespoons chopped parsley **1 bay leaf** **Salt and pepper**	Add parsley, bay leaf, salt, and pepper; bring to boil. Reduce heat; simmer 10 minutes. Add cabbage; cook 20 minutes or until vegetables are tender but not mushy. Adjust seasoning.
Pinch of nutmeg **2 teaspoons chopped dill or 1 teaspoon dillseeds**	Add nutmeg and dill. Remove bay leaf.
3 to 4 frankfurters **Fat for frying** **Fried bread-and-bacon croutons**	For garnish either fry frankfurters and cut in slices, putting a few slices into each serving or prepare fried bread-and-bacon croutons to serve separately.

Yield: 4 to 6 servings.

Pea-Pod Soup

Good to serve when fresh green peas are plentiful.

2 pounds pea pods	Wash pods.
1 onion, peeled, sliced	Put into large kettle with onion, mint, parsley, and stock.
2 to 3 sprigs mint	Bring to boil; cover.
2 to 3 sprigs parsley	Simmer about 40 minutes.
4 cups stock or 2 bouillon cubes and 4 cups water	When outer flesh of pods is tender, rub mixture through sieve.
2 tablespoons margarine	Melt margarine in pan.
1½ tablespoons flour	Stir in flour; cook 2 minutes.
	Add puree; stir until boiling.
Salt and pepper	Add salt, pepper, and sugar to taste.
Sugar	
4 tablespoons cooked green peas (optional)	Add peas.
Chopped mint or mint leaves	Serve sprinkled with a little chopped mint or mint leaves.
	Yield: 4 servings.

Pea-Pod Soup

Whitefish Chowder

Head, skin, and bones of fish **2 cups water**	Wash fish skin, head, and bones in cold water. Put into pan with water.
1 onion, sliced **1 carrot, sliced** **1 bay leaf** **3 or 4 sprigs parsley (or 1 tablespoon dried parsley)** **Salt and pepper**	Add sliced onion, carrot, bay leaf, parsley, salt, and pepper. Bring slowly to boil; skim as necessary. Reduce heat; simmer 15 to 20 minutes. Strain; reserve liquid for chowder.
1 small cube fat salt pork (about 1 inch) or 2 or 3 slices fat bacon	Chop fat salt pork; cook slowly until fat melts. Remove crispy pieces of bacon; reserve for garnish
1 onion, chopped **1 cup diced potatoes** **1 pound fresh cod, haddock, or halibut, filleted** **1 pound fresh cod, haddock, or halibut, filleted**	Add chopped onion to hot fat. Cook gently until tender. Add potatoes and fish stock. Cook 5 to 6 minutes. Add fish chunks. Simmer until potatoes are tender and fish cooked, about 10 minutes.
2 cups milk **¼ teaspoon ground mace or nutmeg** **1 tablespoon chopped fennel** **1 tablespoon chopped parsley**	Bring milk to near boiling point. Add to fish mixture with seasoning and herbs.
2 tablespoons butter	When ready to serve, stir in butter. Serve at once. Yield: 4 to 6 servings.

Whitefish Chowder

Spinach Soup

4 or 5 handfuls fresh spinach (or 1 package frozen)	Wash fresh spinach thoroughly. Drain; shake off excess water.
3 tablespoons butter	Melt butter.
1 onion, chopped fine	Cook onion and spinach gently until spinach has softened and become limp, without browning. If using frozen spinach, allow block to unfreeze completely during this process.
1½ tablespoons flour	Sprinkle in flour; blend smoothly.
4 cups white or vegetable stock (or water and chicken cube)	Add stock. Bring soup to boil, stirring constantly.
3 or 4 parsley sprigs (or 1 tablespoon dried parsley) **1 bay leaf**	Add parsley, bay leaf, salt, and pepper. Reduce heat; simmer 10 to 12 minutes. Do not overcook; this spoils the green color and fresh flavor.
Salt and pepper	Put soup through fine food mill or blend until smooth in electric blender.
Squeeze or 2 of lemon juice	Reheat, adding a little lemon juice. Adjust seasoning.
¼ to ½ teaspoon powdered mace	Add mace.
½ cup cream	Stir in cream just before serving.
2 hard-boiled eggs, sliced **Paprika**	Garnish with slices of hard-boiled egg in each cup; sprinkle with paprika.
Fried bread or bacon croutons	Alternatively, garnish with fried bread or bacon croutons. Yield: 4 to 6 servings.

Spinach Soup

Chicken Chowder

A good way to use the carcass and giblets of a chicken.

Chicken carcass and giblets
3 pints boiling water
1 onion, peeled, sliced
3 stalks celery (with leaves), chopped
1 carrot, peeled, diced
1¼ teaspoon salt

Break up carcass. Put with giblets into large kettle.
Add boiling water, onion, celery, carrot, and 1 teaspoon salt.
Cover; simmer about 1½ hours.

Remove carcass pieces and giblets. Cut off all meat; return to pan.

1 can (1 pound) cream-style corn
1 hard-cooked egg, chopped fine

Add corn; simmer 10 minutes.

Add hard-cooked egg.
Adjust seasoning.

1 cup flour
1 egg, beaten

Sift flour and ¼ teaspoon salt together.
Stir in beaten egg with fork until mixture looks like cornmeal.
Drop in spoonfuls into hot soup a few minutes before serving.

Yield: 5 to 6 servings.

Turkey-Vegetable Soup

1 small onion, chopped
2 tablespoons butter or margarine

Cook onion in butter until tender.

2 cups water
2 chicken bouillon cubes
2 cups diced cooked turkey
½ cup celery tops and pieces
1½ cups diced potatoes
1 cup diced carrots

Add water, bouillon cubes, turkey, and vegetables.
Boil gently, covered, until vegetables are tender.

2½ cups milk
2 tablespoons flour
1 teaspoon salt
⅛ teaspoon pepper

Stir a little milk into flour until mixture is smooth.

Add remaining milk, salt, and pepper.
Add milk mixture to soup.
Simmer, stirring occasionally to prevent sticking, until soup is slightly thickened.

Chicken-Vegetable Soup

Use chicken instead of turkey and chicken broth instead of water and bouillon cubes.

Yield: 6 servings.

Squash Soup

1 large squash	Peel squash. Cut into pieces; remove seeds.
⅜ cup margarine 1 onion, peeled, sliced 1 cup water Bouquet garni Salt and pepper	Melt margarine in pan. Put in squash and onion; cook about 5 minutes, stirring well. Add water, bouquet garni, and a little salt and pepper. Cook until squash is quite soft. Remove bouquet garni. Strain through sieve. Mash squash until smooth. Add to liquid; return all to pan.
3 tablespoons flour 1 cup milk	Blend flour smoothly with milk. Add to squash puree; stir until boiling. Reduce heat; simmer 5 minutes.
1 egg yolk 2 tablespoons light cream or evaporated milk	Mix egg yolk with cream. Stir into soup; reheat, but do not allow to boil. Adjust seasoning.

Serve with croutons of fried or toasted bread.

Yield: 4 servings.

Split-Pea Soup

1 large onion 3 tablespoons fat or drippings	Chop onion. Cook in fat or drippings in large pan until tender.
1½ cups dry split peas 6 cups water 1½ teaspoons salt	Wash and drain split peas. Add water, split peas, and salt to onion. Bring to boil. Lower heat; cover pan. Cook about 2 hours, until thickened. Note: Cook a ham bone or pieces of ham in the soup, if you like. Remove bones; serve meat in soup.

Yield: 6 servings.

Potato Soup

1 large onion, chopped 2 tablespoons butter or margarine	Cook onion in butter until tender.
5 large potatoes, cut into small pieces	Add potatoes and water. Boil gently, covered, 15 minutes or until potatoes are tender.
1 cup water 3 cups milk 2 teaspoons salt Pepper to taste	Mash potatoes. Add milk and seasonings. Heat slowly to serving temperature; stir occasionally to prevent sticking.

Yield: 6 servings.

CHEESE AND EGG DISHES

Cheese Casserole

1 tablespoon butter
1 clove garlic
5 slices white bread,
   buttered, cubed
½ pound cheese, grated

Rub casserole dish with butter and garlic.

Alternate bread with cheese in dish.

4 eggs
2 cups milk
Tabasco sauce to taste
1 teaspoon Worcestershire
   sauce
1 teaspoon dry mustard
Salt and pepper to taste

Beat eggs, milk, Tabasco, Worcestershire, mustard, salt,
   and pepper together.
Pour over layered bread and cheese.
Let stand for 6 hours or more.

Place casserole dish in pan of water.

Bake at 300° F for 1½ hours.

Yield: About 6 servings.

English Monkey

1 cup milk
1 cup bread crumbs
1 cup grated cheddar or
   American cheese
½ teaspoon salt
¼ teaspoon paprika pepper
⅛ teaspoon dry mustard
1 teaspoon Worcestershire
   sauce
1 egg, beaten
4 slices hot buttered toast

Put milk, bread crumbs and cheese into top of double
   boiler. Stir over hot water until cheese has melted.

Add seasonings, Worcestershire sauce, and egg. Cook 1
   minute, stirring all the time, then pour over toast.

Yield: 4 servings.

Egg Pie

Pie Crust

Preheat oven to 400°F.

1½ cups all-purpose flour
¾ teaspoon salt
½ cup shortening
3 tablespoons cold water

Make pie crust in usual way; use half to line 7-inch pie plate. Prick base with fork.

Filling

2 tablespoons margarine
1 onion, peeled, chopped
½ pound tomatoes, peeled, seeded, chopped
1 tablespoon chopped parsley
2 hard-boiled eggs, chopped
2 eggs, beaten
⅛ teaspoon dried or ½ teaspoon fresh chopped chervil (optional)

Heat margarine in pan.
Sauté onion until soft but not browned.
Add tomatoes; cook 2 minutes.
Remove from heat.
Add all other ingredients except milk.
Moisten edges; cover with remaining pastry.
Press edges well together.
Decorate as desired; make 2 slits in top.

3 tablespoons milk

Brush with milk to glaze; let cool.

Bake about 30 minutes or until golden brown.

Yield: 4 or 5 servings.

Creamed Eggs on Toast

¼ cup margarine
¼ cup flour
2 teaspoons Worcestershire sauce
2 teaspoons prepared mustard
1 teaspoon salt
3 cups milk

Melt margarine.
Blend in flour.
Add seasonings.

Gradually stir in milk.
Cook, stirring constantly, until thickened.

8 eggs, hard-cooked, sliced

Add eggs; do not stir. Heat to serving temperature.

6 slices toast

Serve on toast.

Yield: 6 servings.

Curried Eggs on Toast

Omit Worcestershire sauce and mustard.
Cook 2 tablespoons finely chopped onion in margarine.
Stir in flour and ½ or 1 teaspoon curry powder, as desired.

Curried Eggs

Curried Eggs

1 medium-sized onion, peeled, chopped
2 to 3 tablespoons oil
2 tablespoons flour
1 tablespoon curry powder
Salt
2 cups stock or 1 bouillon cube and water
1 large apple, peeled, cored, diced
1 tablespoon Worcestershire sauce
4 hard-boiled eggs

About 2 cups freshly cooked rice

Chutney

Sauté onion in oil until soft but not browned.

Add flour, curry powder, and a little salt. Stir over low heat until mixture forms a smooth paste.
Add stock gradually; stir until boiling.

Add apple and Worcestershire sauce. Cover; simmer gently 15 to 20 minutes.
Add eggs; heat through.

Put rice on large platter.
Arrange eggs and sauce on top.

Serve with chutney and a tossed green salad.

Yield: 4 servings.

Cottage-Cheese Blintzes

¾ cup flour
½ teaspoon salt
½ cup water
½ cup milk (nonfat dry is fine)
2 eggs
1 egg white
1½ tablespoons oil

Sift flour and salt together.

Add water and milk; beat until smooth.

Beat in eggs and egg white thoroughly.

Add 1 tablespoon oil.

Grease a 7-inch frying pan.

Use about ¼ cup batter per crepe (add water if it doesn't spread thinly enough).
Brown on both sides. Makes about 12-15 crepes.

12 ounces cottage cheese
1 egg yolk
1 teaspoon margarine
1 teaspoon vanilla
1 teaspoon nutmeg
Pinch of sugar

Mix cottage cheese, egg yolk, 1 teaspoon margarine, vanilla, nutmeg, and sugar well. Place 1 to 2 tablespoons mixture on crepe; roll up.

½ tablespoon margarine

Melt ½ tablespoon oil and ½ tablespoon margarine in frying pan.
Place several blintzes in pan, seam-side-down.
Fry until lightly brown.
Turn once.
Add more fat as needed.

Plain yogurt
Cinnamon and pinch of sugar (optional)

Top with plain yogurt; sprinkle with cinnamon and sugar.

Yield: about 4 servings.

Bacon and Apple Pie

The cheaper kind of bacon can be used, and if you prefer to use ready prepared pie crust, it still makes an economical supper or luncheon dish.

Preheat oven to 425°F.

½ **pound bacon slices, cut into strips**

Line 8-inch pie pan with bacon strips.

1 large onion, peeled, chopped very fine

Arrange layers of onion and apples on top.

1 pound cooking apples, peeled, cored, sliced thin

2 teaspoons dried sage
Salt and pepper
3 teaspoons sugar

Sprinkle each layer with sage, salt, pepper, and sugar. (Use salt with discretion, depending on saltiness of bacon.)

Pie crust for 8-inch pie
Milk

Cover with pastry; brush with a little milk to glaze.

Bake 25 minutes.
Reduce heat to 350°F. Cover pie with foil if it is browning too quickly; cook 10 to 15 minutes.

Bacon and Apple Pie

Yield: 4 or 5 servings.

Frankfurter Casserole

Frankfurter Casserole

2 tablespoons cooking fat	Heat fat in skillet with tightly fitting lid.
1½ cups diced potatoes	Add potatoes and onion. Cook over low heat about 10
1 cup finely chopped onion	minutes.
2 green peppers, seeded and thinly sliced	Add green peppers and frankfurters; mix well. Cook 5
8 frankfurters, cut in 1 inch slices	minutes.
4 tablespoons water	Add water, salt, and pepper. Cover; cook 10 minutes
Salt and pepper to taste	longer.
	Yield: 4 servings.

Barbecue

1 medium-size onion, chopped	Cook onion in fat until tender.
1 tablespoon fat or oil	Stir in rest of ingredients.
½ cup tomato paste or tomato puree	Heat to boiling.
¼ cup sugar	
2 tablespoons vinegar	
2½ cups cut-up, canned chopped meat or canned luncheon meat	

Serve in buns or on toast, hot cooked bulgur, or rice.

Yield: 6 servings.

Lamb and Rice Loaf

½ small onion	Finely chop onion and green pepper.
½ green pepper	
1 pound ground lamb	Mix all ingredients well. Shape in loaf in baking pan.
1½ cups cooked rice	
1 egg	
1½ teaspoons salt	

Bake at 350°F about 1 hour, until browned.

Yield: 6 servings.

Beef Cabbage Rolls

1 medium-size head cabbage, with loose leaves	Cut hard center core from cabbage. Cook in boiling water to cover about 5 minutes. Cool; separate leaves.
1 pound ground beef	Mix ground beef, rice, onion, egg, cheese, and salt.
½ cup uncooked rice	
1 small onion, chopped	Put 1 tablespoon meat mixture on cabbage leaf. Fold sides of cabbage leaves over toward center; roll up.
1 egg	
½ cup cut-up or grated cheese	
1 tablespoon salt	
3½ cups cooked or canned tomatoes	Place cabbage meat rolls in baking pan. Add tomatoes.
Cinnamon (optional)	Sprinkle with cinnamon (if used).

Bake at 350°F about 1 hour.

Yield: 8 servings.

Beef Casserole

Preheat oven to 375°F.

¼ cup margarine
3 cups diced leftover beef
1 cup thinly sliced onion
1 green pepper, seeded, cut
    into strips

In skillet melt margarine; sauté beef, onions, and green peppers until lightly brown.

¼ pound mushrooms, sliced
4 tomatoes, cut into chunks

Add mushrooms and tomatoes; simmer few minutes.

3 cups thin brown gravy or 1
    can golden mushroom
    soup and 1 soup-can
    water

Add gravy mixture.

4 ounces macaroni

Cook macaroni according to package directions. Drain.

Combine with beef.

½ teaspoon salt
¼ teaspoon pepper
Parmesan cheese, grated

Season to taste with salt and pepper.

Pour into casserole; top with cheese.

Bake 25 to 30 minutes.

Yield: about 4 servings.

Chili Con Carne

1 tablespoon fat or oil
½ pound ground beef
1 medium-size onion,
    chopped
½ green pepper, chopped

Heat fat in large frypan.
Add meat, onion, and green pepper; brown lightly.

1 clove garlic, minced
2 cups tomatoes, cooked or
    1 16-ounce can
3 cups kidney beans, dry,
    cooked, drained (about
    1¼ cups dry)
2 or 3 teaspoons chili
    powder, as desired
1 teaspoon salt

Add remaining ingredients. Cover; simmer about 25 minutes to blend flavors.

To thicken, remove cover during last few minutes of cooking.

Note: Canned, drained kidney beans can be used in this recipe, if preferred.

Yield: 6 servings.

24

Chinese Beef and Vegetables

1 pound round steak, sliced
  very thin (3 inch lengths)
2 tablespoons soy sauce
3 tablespoons oil

Mix meat with 4 teaspoons soy sauce; lightly brown in hot
  oil.

5 tablespoons cornstarch
1 cup chicken broth
1½ teaspoons fresh ginger,
  minced
3 tablespoons sherry

Mix cornstarch with broth.
Stir in remaining soy sauce, ginger and sherry.

8 cups Chinese cabbage
  and/or spinach, cut up

Add greens to browned meat.
Cook briefly until wilted.

Add broth; stir until broth thickens.

Yield: about 4 servings.

Ground Beef Chop Suey

2 cups celery, thin 1-inch
  strips
½ cup sliced onion
1 pound ground beef
1 tablespoon fat or oil

Cook celery, onion, and ground beef in hot fat in large
  frypan about 5 minutes, until meat begins to brown.

2 tablespoons cornstarch
1½ cups water
1 beef bouillon cube
¼ cup soy sauce
½ teaspoon salt
4 cups chopped cabbage

Blend cornstarch with water. Stir into beef mixture. Add
  bouillon cube, soy sauce, and salt.
Cook, stirring constantly, until sauce is thickened and
  clear.

Stir in cabbage. Cook, covered, about 3 minutes, until
  cabbage is tender but still firm.

4 cups rice, cooked (about
  1⅓ cups uncooked)

Serve on rice.

Note: In place of cabbage a 16-ounce can bean sprouts
  can be used. Drain; use liquid in place of part of water.
  Heat only to serving temperature after adding bean
  sprouts.

Chicken Chop Suey

In place of ground beef and beef bouillon cube use 2 cups
  diced, cooked chicken and chicken bouillon cube.

Yield: 6 servings.

Chipped Beef Deluxe

2 tablespoons fat or oil
½ cup celery, chopped
2 tablespoons green pepper, chopped
2 tablespoons onion, chopped

Heat fat.
Add raw vegetables; cook until they begin to brown.

1 10½-ounce can condensed cream of mushroom soup
½ cup water
4-ounce package dried beef

Stir mushroom soup, water, and beef into vegetables. Cook, stirring as needed, until thickened.

2 tablespoons pimiento, chopped
2 hard-cooked eggs, diced

Add pimiento and eggs.

3 cups noodles, cooked (about 6 ounces uncooked)

Serve on Noodles.

Note: In place of mushroom soup and water, you can use 2 cups of milk and ¼ cup flour. Gradually blend milk into flour.

Yield: 6 servings.

Danish Hash

2 large potatoes

Peel and boil potatoes until just tender but not soft. Dice into pieces about ¼ to ½ inch square.

Cook chopped onions in 3 tablespoons fat until tender, about 7 minutes. Remove from pan.

2 cups diced cold meat, preferably beef with ham or bacon

Brown meat for few minutes.
Add potatoes; cook 2 to 3 minutes.

1 large or 2 medium onions, chopped
4 to 5 tablespoons bacon fat or butter

Return onions; cook whole mixture 3 to 4 minutes.

1 to 2 teaspoons Worcestershire sauce
1 teaspoon tomato sauce
Salt and pepper
1 tablespoon chopped parsley

Add Worcestershire, tomato sauce, and seasoning. Sprinkle with parsley; put in ovenproof dish to keep warm.

4 eggs

Fry eggs in remaining fat.

Serve hash at once with 1 fried egg (placed carefully to avoid breaking) on top of each serving.

Yield: 4 servings.

Cottage Pie

2 medium onions, chopped
1 or 2 tablespoons oil
1 to 1½ pounds or 4 to 6
cups diced or ground
cooked beef or lamb
½ to ¾ cup beef stock
Salt and pepper
1 tablespoon chopped mixed
herbs, mainly parsley
Nutmeg
Worcestershire sauce

Preheat oven to 375°F.
Cook onions in oil until golden brown. (Do not overbrown; this will make dish bitter).
Add meat, stock, seasoning, herbs, a grating of nutmeg, and a dash of Worcestershire sauce.

4 to 6 medium sized
potatoes
1 tablespoon butter
Milk

Peel potatoes; boil in salted water until tender. When soft, drain; dry in saucepan.
Mash; beat in 1 tablespoon butter, then a little milk. Be sure not to make puree too soft. Season to taste.

Put meat mixture into ovenproof dish; smooth down. Pile hot potato on top to make slightly domed cover. Rough surface evenly with fork; sprinkle with small pieces of butter.

Bake in oven 30 to 40 minutes, by which time top should be crisp and brown.

As a variation chopped mushrooms or a little chutney can be added to meat mixture.

Yield: 4 to 6 servings.

Cottage Pie

Spaghetti with Meatballs

Salt
½-pound package spaghetti

Bring large pot of water to boil. Add salt. Curl in spaghetti; bring to boil, stirring constantly. Simmer 10 to 15 minutes, until done but still firm. Drain and wash with hot water; drain again.

4 tablespoons butter
Black pepper

Melt 1 tablespoon butter.
Add spaghetti and black pepper; toss. Keep warm.

1 pound ground beef
1 small onion, chopped
3 tablespoons finely chopped parsley, thyme, and marjoram
2 cloves garlic
1 cup fresh white bread crumbs

Mix together ground beef and chopped onion.

Add herbs, 1 crushed garlic clove, and bread crumbs. Season well with salt and black pepper. Shape mixture into small meatballs.

Melt 1 tablespoon butter; fry meatballs until brown. This takes 5 to 7 minutes.

1 onion sliced

1 tablespoon flour
1 can tomatoes
2 teaspoons tomato puree
1 cup stock
1 tablespoon mixed herbs
½ cup grated Parmesan cheese

To make tomato sauce: Melt 2 tablespoons butter. Cook sliced onion and 1 crushed garlic clove 5 minutes.
Mix in flour.
Add tomatoes, puree, stock, herbs, and seasoning.
Bring to boil; simmer 10 to 15 minutes.
Strain sauce; add meatballs. Heat through. Serve with spaghetti.
Serve grated parmesan separately.

Yield: 4 servings

Spaghetti with Meatballs

Yankee Doodle Macaroni

Yankee Doodle Macaroni

3 tablespoons cooking fat
2 cups finely chopped onion
2 cloves garlic, crushed
½ cup sliced mushrooms
1 pound ground beef
1 can (about 1 pound 13 ounces) peeled tomatoes
1 tablespoon chopped parsley
Salt
Pepper

Heat fat in pan.
Add onion, garlic, and mushrooms. Sauté until onion becomes pale yellow in color.

Add meat; stir until it browns.
Add tomatoes, parsley, and seasoning. Cover; simmer about 45 minutes.

1 package (7 to 8 ounces) macaroni
1 to 2 tablespoons margarine

While meat is cooking, cook macaroni in boiling salted water 7 to 10 minutes (or according to package instructions). Drain well; toss in margarine.

Grated Parmesan or sharp cheddar cheese

Turn macaroni onto hot platter; pour meat sauce over. Sprinkle with grated cheese.

Note: Other pasta can be substituted for macaroni.

Yield: 6 to 7 servings.

Monday's Dinner

3 to 4 tablespoons
   margarine
1 tablespoon oil
2 medium onions, peeled
   and finely chopped

Heat 2 tablespoons margarine and the oil in kettle. Put in onions. Sauté few minutes.

1 cup chopped cooked meat
1 small can (6 ounces)
   tomato or mushroom sour
1 tablespoon finely chopped
   parsley
½ bay leaf

Add meat; stir about 5 minutes.
Add soup, parsley and bay leaf. Cover; simmer 15 minutes.

1 cup cooked vegetables
   (peas, carrots, potatoes,
   etc.)
1 cup stock (or gravy)
Salt and pepper

Add vegetables and stock; heat through. Season to taste. Remove bay leaf.

1 package (7 to 8 ounces)
   macaroni

Cook macaroni; drain.
Toss in 1 to 2 tablespoons margarine. Turn onto large platter. Pour meat and vegetable mixture on top.

Grated Parmesan or sharp
   cheddar cheese (optional)

If you wish, sprinkle cheese on top.

Yield: 6 or 7 servings.

Monday's Dinner

Moussaka

Preheat oven to 350°F.

2 large eggplants, peeled, cut into ¼-inch slices
Salt

Put slices of eggplant into colander. Sprinkle with salt; let drain.

5 tablespoons oil
1 onion, peeled and finely chopped

Heat 1 tablespoon oil in skillet.
Add onion. Sauté until just beginning to brown.

½ pound ground beef
Pepper
Pinch of thyme
1 large tomato, peeled, seeded and chopped

Add meat. Cook together, stirring, until meat has browned. Season with salt, pepper, and a pinch of thyme.

Add tomato.

Rinse and dry eggplant. Sauté in 4 tablespoons heated oil until golden brown.

Cracker crumbs

Cover bottom of greased casserole with thin layer of cracker crumbs. Arrange layer of eggplant slices on top.

1 egg, separated

Beat egg white stiff. Fold into meat mixture with 2 teaspoons cracker crumbs. Adjust seasoning to taste.

Arrange layer of meat mixture over eggplant. Repeat layers, finishing with eggplant.

½ cup milk
¼ cup grated cheese

Combine egg yolk, milk and cheese. Pour into casserole. Cook 30 minutes.

Chopped parsley

Sprinkle with parsley before serving.

Yield: 4 to 6 servings.

Beef Pot Roast

⅓ cup flour
2 teaspoons salt
¼ teaspoon pepper
4 pounds chuck or round roast, boneless
2 tablespoons fat or oil
About ½ cup water

Mix flour and seasonings; coat meat with mixture.
Heat fat in heavy pan.
Brown meat on all sides.
Add water as needed to prevent overbrowning. Cover tightly.

Cook over low heat or in oven at 350°F until tender. Cooking time will be about 2½ to 3½ hours, depending on thickness of meat.

Notes: Trim excess fat from meat. It can be used to provide fat needed for browning meat.
Brown meat without flour coating, if preferred.

Yield: 12 or more servings.

Stuffed Green Peppers

3 large green peppers

Halve peppers lengthwise; remove stems, seeds, and membranes.

2 teaspoons salt
Boiling water

Add 2 teaspoons salt to enough boiling water to cover peppers; boil peppers 5 minutes. Drain.

1 pound ground beef
1½ cups cooked rice
2 tablespoons finely chopped celery
2 tablespoons finely chopped onion
¼ cup chili sauce
2 teaspoons salt
¼ teaspoon pepper
1 egg

Combine other ingredients except cheese; mix well. Fill pepper halves with mixture; place in ½ inch hot water in baking pan.
Bake uncovered at 350°F 45 to 55 mintues.

2 tablespoons shredded Cheddar cheese

Sprinkle cheese over peppers; bake 5 minutes or just until cheese melts.

Yield: 6 servings.

Sweet-and-Sour Beef

1 tablespoon shortening
2 pounds lean stewing beef, cubed

Melt shortening in large skillet; brown beef on all sides.

½ teaspoon salt
2 cups canned tomatoes
⅓ cup brown sugar
⅓ cup vinegar
½ cup finely chopped onion
½ bay leaf

Add salt, tomatoes, brown sugar, vinegar, onion, and bay leaf.
Cover skillet; lower heat. Let simmer about 2 hours or until beef is tender.

1 green pepper, cut into thin strips

Add pepper strips to beef; cook 10 minutes more to blend all flavors.

Serve over hot rice or with noodles.

Yield: 6 to 8 servings.

Spicy Frankfurter Rolls

12 Frankfurters	Cook frankfurters, turning occasionally.
1 cup butter or margarine **1 small onion, peeled, finely chopped** **2 tablespoons finely chopped parsley** **2 teaspoons prepared mustard** **2 tablespoons tomato catsup** **Pepper**	Soften butter. Add onion, parsley, mustard, catsup and pepper to taste. Mix well.
12 soft rolls	Split rolls. Spread with butter mixture. Put on coolest part of barbecue to heat through. Place frankfurter in each roll. Yield: 12 rolls.

Super Franks

8 to 10 slices white bread	Trim crusts from bread (save crusts to use for bread crumbs). Flatten each slice of bread with rolling pin.
¼ cup prepared yellow mustard **2 tablespoons catsup** **2 tablespoons crunchy peanut butter**	Combine mustard, catsup, and peanut butter; spread on bread.
1 pound frankfurters (8 to 10) **Melted butter**	Place a frankfurter diagonally across each slice of bread. Wrap corners of bread up over frankfurters; fasten with wooden picks. Brush outside of bread lightly with melted butter. Bake at 400°F 15 to 20 minutes, until frankfurters are heated and bread lightly toasted. Yield: 4 or 5 servings.

Sautéed Chicken Livers

1 pound chicken livers **4 tablespoons flour** **4 tablespoons margarine** **1 cup chicken broth** **2 tablespoons sherry (optional)** **½ teaspoon thyme** **Salt** **Pepper**	Dredge livers in flour; sauté in margarine until brown. Take livers out; keep warm. Put remaining flour in pan; stir a minute. Remove from heat. Add chicken broth. Stir over heat, scraping up flour, until sauce thickens. (Add sherry, if desired). Add seasonings. Return livers to pan; heat through. Yield: about 4 servings.

Ham Leftovers Delish

1 cup mashed potatoes
1 cup ground cooked ham
¼ teaspoon lemon pepper
Flour for batter

Mix mashed potatoes, ham, and lemon pepper together.
Form into flat cakes about 3 inches in diameter.
Dip each cake lightly in flour; set aside.

2 or more tablespoons fat
for frying

Melt fat in medium skillet. Lightly brown each cake on
both sides. The ham cakes can be kept warm in the oven
until ready to serve them.

Yield: 4 to 6 servings.

Ham and Pasta Savory

2 cups shell pasta
1 cup cottage cheese, sieved

Cook pasta about 12 minutes, or follow package instructions. Drain well; combine with cheese.

4 tablespoons margarine
1 cup cooked diced ham
Salt
Cayenne pepper
Chopped parsley

Melt margarine in pan.
Add ham; heat through.
Add pasta and cheese; season to taste with salt and
cayenne.
Put into hot serving dish; sprinkle with parsley. Serve with
tossed green salad.

Yield: 4 servings.

Irish Stew

1½ to 2 pounds rib or
shoulder chops of lamb

Trim excess fat off chops.

4 medium potatoes
2 to 3 medium onions
1 tablespoon chopped
parsley
½ teaspoon chopped thyme
1 small bay leaf

Cut potatoes and onions into quarters or thick slices.
Place meat and vegetables in thick stew pot in layers,
starting and ending with layer of potatoes. Sprinkle
herbs and seasoning on each layer.
Add 2 cups water. Cover tightly with lid or foil.
Simmer stew over gentle heat (or cook in 250°F oven) 2 to
2½ hours. Shake pan from time to time to prevent stew
from sticking. Toward end of cooking time check liquid
in pan. Consistency should be thick and creamy but not
dry, so add a little more liquid if necessary.

Sometimes 4 carrots and 1 turnip are added to this stew,
but this would not be accepted in Ireland as true Irish
stew.

Yield: 4 servings.

Ham Gougere

Preheat oven to 375°F.

1 tablespoon butter
1 onion

Melt 1 tablespoon butter. Cook sliced onion until soft.

½ cup mushrooms

Add mushrooms; cook 1 minute.

½ tablespoon flour
1 tablespoon tomato puree
½ cup stock
1 tablespoon sherry
½ to 1 cup diced cooked ham (or other meat)
1 tablespoon chopped herbs

Add ½ tablespoon flour. When well mixed, add tomato puree and stock. Stir until it boils; cook until it has thickened a little.

Add sherry, diced ham, and herbs. Allow to cool slightly before spooning into dish.

½ cup all-purpose flour
½ cup water
¼ cup butter

Sift warmed all-purpose flour.

In pan with sloping sides heat ½ cup water and ¼ cup butter. When butter has melted, bring mixture to boil. As soon as it boils remove from heat; add all flour at once. Beat hard with wooden spoon until mxiture forms ball in bottom of pan. Let cool.

2 eggs

Beat eggs. When mixture is cool, add egg by degrees, beating hard between each addition. The final mixture should be shiny and smooth and hold its shape. A little egg should be saved.

4 tablespoons grated Cheddar cheese
½ teaspoon dried mustard

Add cheddar cheese and mustard.

Butter dish about 3 inches deep. Arrange pastry in ring around outside of dish. Put mixture in center; brush top with saved beaten egg to give shine.

2 tablespoons grated Parmesan cheese
2 tablespoons cornflake crumbs

Sprinkle top with Parmesan cheese and cornflake crumbs.

Bake in oven 30 to 45 minutes for large dish or 15 to 20 minutes for small.

2 teaspoons chopped parsley

Sprinkle top with chopped parsley.

Yield: 4 servings.

Ham Gougere

Veal and Mushroom Pancakes

1¼ cups flour
Salt and pepper
2 eggs, beaten
1 egg yolk, beaten
1½ cups milk

Preheat broiler.
Sift 1 cup flour with salt and pepper into bowl.
Make hollow in center; drop in beaten eggs and 3 to 4 tablespoons milk. Mix eggs and milk together with spoon before gradually drawing in flour.
Add 6 tablespoons milk as mixture thickens. When smooth and like thick cream, beat about 5 minutes.
Stir in 2 teaspoons melted butter and 3 tablespoons milk. Leave batter in covered bowl about ½ hour before using.

3 tablespoons butter
1 cup mushrooms

Melt about 2 tablespoons butter; cook sliced mushrooms in covered pan 3 to 4 minutes. Remove from stove.
Stir in scant tablespoon flour.
Add ½ cup milk. Bring slowly to boil.

1½ cups chopped cooked veal
½ cup corn
1 tablespoon chopped parsley
A little cream
Pinch of mace or ground nutmeg
A little oil

Add chopped meat, corn, parsley, mace, seasoning, and cream. Keep warm while cooking pancakes.

Test thickness of batter, which should just coat back of spoon. If too thick, add remaining milk; stir well. Grease 5 to 6 inch pancake or frying pan with a little oil. When hot, pour in enough batter to coat pan thinly. When browned on one side, turn, cook on other side. Pile up; keep warm.

Put spoonful filling in center of each pancake; roll up. Arrange in overlapping rows in ovenproof dish.

3 tablespoons grated Parmesan cheese
1½ tablespoons melted butter

Sprinkle with grated cheese; spoon over melted butter.

Broil until golden brown.

Yield: 4 to 6 servings.

Picture on opposite page

Veal and Mushroom Pancakes

Scotch Collops

4 tablespoons cooking fat
2 onions, peeled and
    chopped

Heat fat in pan, add onion; sauté until transparent.

2 carrots, peeled and diced
1½ pounds ground beef
1½ cups stock (or water)
2 tablespoons oatmeal
1 tablespoon tomato
    ketchup
Nutmeg

Add carrots and meat; cook 5 minutes, stirring frequently.

Add stock, oatmeal, tomato ketchup, salt, pepper and a
    dash of nutmeg to taste.
Bring to boil, cover; simmer 15 minutes.

Dumplings

2 cups all purpose flour
¼ teaspoon salt
1½ teaspoons baking
    powder
½ cup margarine

To make dumplings: Sift flour, salt and baking powder, cut
    in fat; mix to a soft but not sticky dough with cold
    water. Shape into small balls with floured hands; put into
    pan after first 15 minutes' cooking.

Cook 10 minutes; put lid on pan, cook 10 more minutes.

Yield: 4 to 5 servings.

Lamb-Stuffed Dolmas

8 to 12 medium-size green
   cabbage leaves

2 to 3 tablespoons butter
1 pound lean ground lamb
1 onion, chopped fine
1 tablespoon flour
2 tablespoons tomato puree
1 tablespoon chopped
   parsley
1 cup cooked rice
¼ teaspoon mixed spice
Salt
Pepper
2 cups stock
2 tablespoons seasoned flour

2 cups tomato sauce or
   brown gravy

Preheat oven to 350°F.
Put cabbage leaves into pan of boiling salted water. Cook
   2 to 3 minutes. Drain; rinse in cold water; let dry.

Heat butter; cook beef and onion until beef is brown.

Sprinkle in flour; stir well.
Add tomato puree, chopped parsley, rice, mixed spice,
   seasoning and about ½ cup stock. Bring to boil; cook 5
   minutes. Cool slightly. Put spoonful on center of each
   cabbage leaf; roll up neatly, tucking in ends to hold in
   stuffing while cooking.

Roll in seasoned flour and place in casserole, packing
   them tightly together.
Pour over 1 cup stock to cover half of Dolmas.
Put lid on casserole.

Cook 45 minutes until tender, adding more stock if
   necessary. Serve with a tomato sauce or brown gravy.

Yield: 4 servings.

Lamb Hot Pot

2 to 3 tablespoons oil
1 to 1½ pounds lean lamb
   neck or shoulder slices

2 onions
4 potatoes, sliced thick
2 carrots, sliced thick
2 stalks celery, sliced thick
1 small can tomatoes (or 4
   to 5 tablespoons tomato
   puree)
1 cup mushrooms
2 cups water or stock
2 tablespoons herbs
1 bay leaf
Salt
Pepper

Preheat oven to 350°F.
Heat oil; brown meat quickly on both sides. Put into deep
   casserole; keep warm.

Cook onions, carrots, celery, and potatoes in oil a few
   minutes.

Add drained tomatoes or tomato puree and mushrooms.
   Pour over meat.

Moisten with 2 cups water or stock.
Sprinkle herbs over top.

Add bay leaf and seasoning.
Put in oven about 1 hour or until meat is tender.

Yield: 4 servings.

Meat Croquettes

2 tablespoons margarine
2 tablespoons flour
¾ cup milk
Salt
Pepper
2 tablespoons grated cheese

Make thick sauce with margarine, flour, and milk.
Add seasoning and grated cheese. Let cool a little.

2 to 2½ cups chopped
  cooked meat
1 egg yolk
1 tablespoon chopped
  parsley
½ teaspoon mixed herbs

Combine meat, egg yolk, parsley, and herbs with sauce.
Add extra seasoning as required.
Mix well. Chill.

Bread crumbs
Oil for frying

Divide into 8 portions. Shape into croquettes. Coat well
  with bread crumbs. Chill again if convenient. Fry in hot
  oil until brown and crisp.

Yield: 4 servings.

Meat Patties

½ pound boneless veal
½ pound boneless pork
1 medium onion, grated
3 tablespoons flour
1½ cups club soda
1 egg
1 teaspoon salt
¼ teaspoon pepper

Have butcher grind meats together twice.

Mix onion with meat. Add flour; mix well. Electric beater
  can be used.
Gradually add club soda; beat until meat is light.
Add beaten egg, salt, and pepper. Cover bowl; refrigerate
  at least 1 hour, so meat can be handled easily.

Shape meat into 4-inch rectangles, 1 inch thick.

6 tablespoons butter or
  vegetable oil

Melt butter in large skillet; add meat patties a few at a
  time. Cook each batch at least 6 to 8 minutes per side.
  Since pork is in mixture, meat must be cooked all the
  way through. Finished patties will be brown on outside,
  with no tinge of pink in center.

Yield: 8 to 10 patties.

Pork-Vegetable Stew

1 pound boneless pork shoulder	Cut meat in small pieces. Brown in large greased pan.
1 medium-size onion 3 medium-size carrots	Slice onions and carrots. Add to meat.
2½ cups water 1 teaspoon salt	Stir in water and salt. Bring to boil. Lower heat. Cover; boil slowly about 45 minutes, until meat and carrots are tender.
1 cup uncooked macaroni 2 cups cooked or canned green beans, undrained	Stir in macaroni and beans. Cover; boil gently about 10 minutes until macaroni is tender, stirring once in a while to keep from sticking. Add water during cooking if mixture seems dry. Yield: 6 servings.

Creole Beef Stew

The flavor of this stew is improved if made the day before and then re-heated.

2 tablespoons oil 1½ to 2 pounds chuck steak or shoulder of beef	Heat oil in heavy skillet, put in meat, cut into cubes; brown on all sides. Remove meat from pan.
2 onions, peeled and thinly sliced	Add onions to fat remaining in pan, sauté until browned.
1 clove garlic, crushed Black pepper ⅛ teaspoon thyme ⅛ teaspoon marjoram A dash of cayenne pepper 1 small bay leaf 1 teaspoon wine vinegar 1 can tomato sauce (8 ounces) 1 cup water ½ teaspoon sugar	Add all other ingredients, stir until boiling.
	Return meat to pan, cover; simmer over very low heat about 2 hours. Remove bay leaf, adjust seasoning. Serve with potatoes (or rice) and a green vegetable. Yield: 4 servings.

POULTRY

Chicken-Cereal Casserole

Preheat oven to 375°F.

Filling

1 tablespoon finely chopped onion

Cook onion in fat in 2-quart saucepan until tender.

2 or 3 tablespoons chicken fat, butter, or margarine
¼ cup flour, unsifted
¾ teaspoon salt (omit if salted broth is used)

Blend in flour, salt, and pepper.

⅛ teaspoon pepper
1 cup chicken broth
1 cup milk, whole or skim

Slowly stir in broth and milk.
Cook over moderate heat until thickened, stirring constantly.

1 (10-ounce) package peas and carrots, frozen
1½ cups diced cooked chicken (or canned chicken)

Add peas and carrots; cook over low heat, stirring occasionally, 5 minutes.
Add chicken. Pour into 1½-quart casserole.

Topping

½ to 1 cup crushed corn or wheat flakes

Combine topping ingredients; mix. Spread over chicken mixture.

½ teaspoon poultry seasoning
1 tablespoon minced parsley
3 tablespoons chopped pimiento
2 or 3 tablespoons butter or margarine

Bake until filling bubbles and topping is crisp, 20 to 30 minutes.
Yield: 6 servings.

Chicken Cream

Preheat oven to 375°F.

4 cups cooked chicken
2 cups fresh bread crumbs

Grind chicken; mix with fresh bread crumbs.

4 tablespoons butter
2 tablespoons flour
1 cup milk

Make cream sauce: Melt 2 tablespoons butter; blend in
    flour.
Add milk gradually.
When smooth, bring to boil, stirring constnatly. Boil 2 to 3
    minutes.

¼ teaspoon ground mace or
   nutmeg
1 tablespoon chopped
   parsley
1 egg, beaten

Add mace and parsley.

Let cool slightly. Add sauce to chicken mixture. Stir well,
    adding remaining butter and beaten egg. Season well.
Put in buttered ovenproof dish, allowing room for chicken
    cream to rise slightly.
Cook in oven 30 to 35 minutes.

Yield: 4 to 6 servings.

Chicken-Grits Croquettes

2 cups cooked grits
2 cups finely chopped
  cooked chicken, meat, or
  fish
2 tablespoons chopped
  onion
1 teaspoon salt
Pepper to taste
1 teaspoon Worcestershire
  sauce

Combine grits, chicken, onion, salt, pepper, and Worcester-
    shire sauce. Chill.

Fine dry bread crumgs
1 egg, beaten

Shape mixture into balls or other shape for 12 croquettes.
    Roll in bread crumbs; dip in egg. Roll again in bread
    crumbs.

Fat or oil for deep frying

Heat fat in frypan.
Cook croquettes in heated fat, turning once to brown each
    side.

Yield: 6 servings.

Curried Chicken

2 small chickens, about 3 pounds each	Cut each chicken into pieces.
1 medium onion, chopped **⅓ cup margarine**	Brown onion in margarine in large skillet. Remove onion. Brown chicken in same fat. Replace onion.
1 light tablespoon curry powder	Add curry powder.
3 cups boiling water **2 teaspoons salt**	Pour boiling water over chicken. Add salt. Simmer until chicken is tender, about 30 minutes.
¼ cup flour	Mix flour with ¼ cup chicken liquid; add to chicken. Stir until thick and smooth.

Serve chicken piping hot on bed of rice.

Yield: 6 or more servings.

Curried Chicken

Chicken–Peach Casserole

Preheat oven to 375°F.

1 frying chicken (about 3½ pounds) or 6 to 8 chicken joints

Disjoint and skin chicken.

2 tablespoons butter or margarine
1 tablespoon oil

Heat butter and oil in skillet.
Brown chicken pieces on all sides; cover.
Reduce heat; cook about 10 minutes.
Remove chicken; arrange in large casserole.

1 large onion, peeled, sliced
1 green pepper, seeded, cut into strips

Sauté onion and pepper in remaining fat until onion is transparent.

1 large can (about 30 ounces) sliced peaches

Drain peaches; reserve syrup.

1 tablespoon cornstarch
1 tablespoon soy sauce
3 tablespoons white-wine vinegar
2 tomatoes, peeled, thickly sliced

Mix cornstarch smoothly with soy sauce and vinegar.
Add 1 cup peach syrup; pour into skillet. Stir until boiling; boil until clear.

Add peaches and tomatoes.
Pour contents of skillet over chicken.
Cover casserole.
Cook 30 to 40 minutes. Remove lid for last 5 minutes.

Adjust seasoning.

Serve with wild rice to which some cooked green peas and a few strips of red pepper have been added.
Yield: 6 servings.

Chicken-Peach Casserole

Chicken à la King

1 cup frozen green peas
2 tablespoons finely
    chopped onion
¼ cup chopped green
    pepper
⅓ cup boiling water

Cook peas, onion, and green pepper in boiling water in covered pan 5 minutes. Drain; save liquid.

⅔ cup flour
1 cup cold milk

Blend flour with milk.

2 cups chicken broth
2 teaspoons salt
Pepper to taste
½ teaspoon poultry
    seasoning
2 cups diced cooked chicken
    or turkey
1 can (4 ounces) mushroom
    stems and pieces, drained,
    chopped
1 tablespoon chopped
    pimiento

Combine vegetable cooking liquid, broth, and seasonings.
Slowly stir in flour mixture. Bring to boil, stirring constantly; cook 1 minute.
Add chicken, cooked vegetables, mushrooms, and pimiento; heat thoroughly.

Cooked rice, toast, or
    biscuits

Serve on rice, toast, or biscuits.
Note: Two chicken bouillon cubes and 2 cups hot water can be used to make broth. Decrease salt to 1 teaspoon.

Yield: 6 servings.

Chicken–Rice Loaf

2 to 3 slices enriched bread

Tear bread in pieces; make 2 cups soft bread crumbs in blender.
Turn into bowl with chicken and rice.

4 cups diced cooked or
    canned chicken
1 cup cooked rice
2 cups chicken broth or 2
    chicken bouillon cubes
    dissolved in 2 cups water

Add broth.

2 canned pimientos
1 cup milk
4 eggs
1 slice onion
1½ teaspoons salt
½ teaspoon pepper
¼ teaspoon thyme

Place remaining ingredients in blender container. Blend until pimiento is chopped.
Stir into mixture in bowl.
Pour into greased 11 × 7 × 2-inch baking dish.

Bake in 325°F oven 1 hour until mixture does not adhere to knife.

Yield: 6 to 8 servings.

Chicken Sorrento

Chicken Sorrento

1 chicken (3 to 3½ pounds)
Flour
Salt and pepper

Preheat oven to 350°F.
Cut chicken into pieces; coat with flour to which a little salt and pepper have been added.

3 tablespoons oil
⅓ cup rice

Heat oil in skillet; brown chicken on all sides. Remove.
Put rice into skillet; stir over low heat until rice is brown.

Put onion and orange through food grinder, using coarse blade.
Mix in rice.

1 large onion, peeled
1 orange, cut in half and
seeded but not peeled
½ cup milk
1 cup water
3 tablespoons chopped
pimiento
¼ teaspoon thyme
Pinch of sugar
Pinch of cayenne pepper

Put onion, orange, and rice mixture into casserole. Arrange chicken on top.
Add milk, water, a little seasoning and all other ingredients; cover.

Cook in oven 1 to 1¼ hours. Adjust seasoning to taste before serving.

Yield: 5 or 6 servings.

46

Savory Chicken and Rice

⅓ cup flour
1 teaspoon salt
¼ teaspoon pepper

In paper or plastic bag combine flour with 1 teaspoon salt and ¼ teaspoon pepper.
Shake chicken, a few pieces at a time, in flour mixture.

2½ to 3 pounds frying chicken, cut into pieces
¼ cup shortening or oil

In large, heavy frypan brown chicken in hot oil over medium heat until golden brown.

1 cup uncooked white rice
1 (10½-ounce) can (1¼ cups) condensed cream of chicken or cream of mushroom soup
1 tablespoon instant minced onion or ¼ cup chopped onion
1 teaspoon salt
¾ teaspoon poultry seasoning or ground sage
½ cup chopped or sliced celery
2 cups water

Combine remaining ingredients in large mixing bowl, mixing well. Pour over chicken in frypan; cover.

Simmer over low heat 55 to 65 minutes, until chicken and rice are tender.

Yield: about 6 servings.

Barbecued Drumsticks

½ cup butter or salad oil
1 medium onion, chopped
1 clove garlic, minced
½ cup lemon juice
⅓ cup Worcestershire sauce
¼ teaspoon Tabasco
1½ cups water
¾ cup catsup
1 teaspoon salt
¾ teaspoon pepper
1 teaspoon monosodium glutamate
1 to 2 tablespoons sugar
1 teaspoon chili powder
¼ teaspoon oregano
12 chicken drumsticks, cooked

Heat butter; add onion and garlic; simmer 2 minutes.
Add remaining ingredients, except chicken. Cover; simmer 10 minutes. Toward end of cooking, thin down sauce, if necessary, with a little water.

Arrange drumsticks in baking dish. Brush sauce over drumsticks. Set aside remaining sauce.

Cover; bake in 375°F oven 15 minutes. Remove cover; baste with remaining sauce. Bake 10 minutes.

Yield: 6 servings.

Chicken Provencal

Long, slow cooking improves the flavor of this dish, so a small stewing fowl is very suitable.

	Preheat oven to 325°F.
1 small stewing fowl	Cut fowl into neat pieces.
Salt and pepper 1 tablespoon cornstarch	Mix salt and pepper with cornstarch; dredge chicken well.
¼ cup butter or margarine	Heat butter in sauté pan. Brown chicken; remove to casserole.
3 small onions, peeled, halved 4 small carrots, peeled, quartered 1 clove garlic, crushed	Add vegetables and garlic to remaining fat with any remaining cornstarch. Cook a few minutes.
4 tablespoons red wine 1 cup chicken broth or water	Add wine and broth; stir until boiling. Pour over chicken. Cover tightly.
	Cook 2½ to 3 hours.
A few black olives	Just before serving, adjust seasoning and add olives.
	Yield: 4 to 5 servings.

Turkey Hash

2 tablespoons margarine 2 tablespoons flour	Melt margarine; stir in flour. Cook and stir until mixture bubbles a bit. Remove from heat.
½ cup milk (nonfat dry milk can be used) ¾ cup canned chicken broth or 1 chicken bouillon cube dissolved in 6 ounces hot water	Stir in milk and broth. Cook, stirring constantly, until smooth and thickened.
Grated rind of ½ lemon Dash of mace	Stir in lemon rind and mace.
¼ pound sliced mushrooms 1 cup diced cooked turkey	Add mushrooms and turkey; keep over low heat until thoroughly heated.
Salt and pepper	Season to taste with salt and pepper.
2 pimientos, cut up	Just before serving, add pimientos.
Chopped parsley	Sprinkle with parsley.
Hot cooked rice	Serve with rice.
	Yield: about 4 servings.

Turkey au Gratin

	Preheat broiler.
3 tablespoons butter	Melt butter; cook onion until tender.
1 onion, chopped	
2 to 3 large mushrooms, chopped	Add mushrooms; cook 1 minute.
2½ tablespoons flour	Sprinkle in flour; blend well.
1½ cups stock	Pour on stock; bring to boil, stirring constantly.
2 to 3 cups chopped cooked turkey (or other poultry or game)	Add turkey and vegetables or noodles. Stir well into sauce.
1 to 2 cups cooked vegetables (peas, beans, corn, chopped carrots, pimiento, etc.) or 1 cup cooked noodles	
1 tablespoon chopped parsley and thyme	Add herbs and cream.
3 to 4 tablespoons thick cream	
4 to 5 tablespoons grated cheddar cheese	Turn into buttered baking dish; sprinkle thickly with grated cheese and a little paprika. Broil until crisp and brown all over.
Paprika	

Yield: 4 to 6 servings.

Turkey Casserole

This should have a really zippy flavor, but use chili peppers with direction: they are very hot.

	Preheat oven to 350°F.
1 tablespoon cooking fat or oil	Heat fat in pan; sauté onion until it begins to color.
2 tablespoons finely chopped onion	
1 can condensed mushroom soup	Add soup, pimiento, and chili pepper.
1 canned pimiento, chopped	
1 teaspoon pickled hot green chili pepper, deseeded, finely chopped	
1 cup cooked diced turkey	Arrange layer of turkey, noodles, and soup mixture in casserole.
Salt and pepper	Sprinkle lightly with salt, pepper, and cheese.
2½ cups cooked noodles (about 5 ounces uncooked)	Repeat layers; sprinkle remaining cheese on top; bake 30 to 40 minutes.
½ cup grated sharp cheese	

Yield: 4 servings.

Turkey-Leg Pot Roast

⅓ cup flour
2 teaspoons salt
¼ teaspoon pepper

Mix flour, salt, and pepper. Use to coat meat.

About ⅓ cup fat or oil
4 to 5 pounds turkey-leg
   quarters

Heat fat in large, heavy frypan of other heavy pan over
   moderate heat. Brown turkey in hot fat on skin side first,
   then on other side.
Drain off fat.

1 cup water

Add water; cover tightly.
Simmer until meat is tender, about 2½ hours.
Add a little water during cooking, if needed, to prevent
   sticking.

Note: Instead of simmering, the browned turkey can be
   baked in covered pan at 350°F about 2½ hours.

Yield: 6 servings.

Braised Turkey Legs or Wings.

In place of turkey-leg quarters, use 2½ to 3 pounds turkey
   drumsticks, thighs, or wings.
Use ½ teaspoon salt per pound of turkey.
Small, young legs and wings will cook in about 1¼ hours.
Larger, more mature ones will take about 2½ hours.

Yield: 6 servings.

Turkey–Pasta Medley

1½ cups shell pasta

Cook pasta in boiling salted water about 10 minutes or
   follow package instructions; drain well.

1 small onion, peeled,
   chopped
4 tablespoons margarine

Sauté onion in 2 tablespoons margarine until soft.

2 tablespoons flour
2 chicken bouillon cubes
2 cups hot water
1 cup diced cooked turkey
   or chicken
½ cup chopped cooked
   bacon
1 cup cooked mixed
   vegetables

Make a sauce with remaining 2 tablespoons margarine,
   flour, and hot water in which bouillon cubes have been
   dissolved. Cook 2 minutes.
Add pasta and remaining ingredients. Add seasoning as
   required; heat through, about 5 minutes.

Yield: 5 or 6 servings.

Turkey Sukiyaki

3 tablespoons oil
1 cup diced green pepper
1 cup diagonally sliced
celery
1 cup diced green onions
with tops
2 cups diced cooked turkey
¼ cup soy sauce

Heat oil in medium skillet.
Add vegetables; cook, stirring, over medium heat 5 minutes
or until vegetables are tender but not mushy.

Add turkey and soy sauce; stir until mixed and heated
through.

Serve over piping-hot rice.

Yield: 4 to 6 servings.

Turkey Sukiyaki

Turkey and Mushroom Croquettes

5 tablespoons butter

4 tablespoons flour for sauce

Make thick sauce: Melt 4 tablespoons butter; add flour.

½ cup strong turkey or chicken stock

½ cup milk

Add stock and milk; bring to boil. Cook until thick and smooth.

Salt and pepper

Pinch of mace

Small pinch of cayenne pepper

1 tablespoon chopped parsley

Add seasonings and parsley; let cool.

3 to 4 tablespoons chopped mushrooms

Cook mushrooms in 1 tablespoon butter.

A little lemon juice

2 cups chopped cooked turkey

Sprinkle with lemon juice. Add turkey.

1 egg yolk, beaten

Add sauce; stir well. When almost cold, add egg yolk. Put mixture into refrigerator to chill and set.

½ cup seasoned flour

2 eggs, beaten with 1 teaspoon oil

1 to 1½ cups dried white bread crumbs

Divide mixture into 12 equal portions. Shape each into small roll with floured fingers. Roll in seasoned flour, coating ends carefully.

Brush all over with beaten egg, then cover thickly with bread crumbs.

Fat for deep frying

Heat fat to 390°F or smoking-hot. Fry 4 croquettes at a time until well browned. Drain well.

Serve at once with a piquant brown or tomato sauce.

Yield: 4 to 6 servings.

FISH

Fish Cakes

1 egg
1 tablespoon lemon juice
1 onion, minced fine
2 tablespoons prepared
   mustard
½ teaspoon salt
¼ teaspoon pepper
1 teaspoon parsley flakes
1 pound cooked fish, boned
   and flaked
¼ cup cornflake crumbs (at
   least)

Fat for deep frying

Mix egg, lemon juice, onion, and seasonings in bowl. Toss with flaked fish.

Add enough cornflake crumbs to shape fish cakes easily. Roll each cake in extra crumbs to coat outside.

Heat fat in medium skillet; fry cakes until crisp and brown on outside. Drain on paper towels, then place on heated platter.

Yield: 4 to 6 servings.

Fish Cakes

Cod Curry

2 pounds cod fillets or other
  fish fillets, fresh or frozen
1 cup thinly sliced celery
1 cup thinly sliced onion
1 tablespoon melted fat
  or oil
1 teaspoon curry powder
1 teaspoon salt
Dash of pepper
¾ cup skim milk

Paprika

Thaw frozen fillets. Skin fillets; place in single layer in
  greased baking dish, 12 × 8 × 2 inches.
Cook celery and onion in fat 5 minutes.
Stir in seasonings and milk. Spread over fish.

Bake in 350°F oven 25 to 30 minutes or until fish flakes
  easily when tested with fork.

Sprinkle with paprika.

Yield: 6 servings.

Fish and Batter

¼ cup margarine

4 fillets cod, haddock, or
  flounder
Juice of ½ lemon

Preheat oven to 435°F.
Grease deep ovenproof dish or casserole with some of
  margarine.
Wash and dry fish; arrange in dish, skin-side-downward.
  Melt remaining; pour over fish.
Add lemon juice and seasoning.
Cover; bake 15 minutes.

1 cup flour
¼ teaspoon salt
1 egg
1 cup milk and water
  (½ and ½)
½ cup grated dry cheese

While fish is cooking, make batter. Sift flour and salt into
  bowl. Make a well in center; drop in egg.

Add half of liquid; stir until smooth. Add rest of liquid.
  When quite smooth, beat very thoroughly.
Add cheese; beat another minute.

When fish has baked 15 minutes, pour batter over it.
Bake 20 minutes longer, or until batter is well risen and
  brown.

Yield: 4 servings.

VEGETABLES

Butter Beans

2 pounds small butter beans
½ cup water
2 tablespoons bacon
  drippings
1 teaspoon seasoned salt
1 onion, cut in half
½ teaspoon pepper
1 clove garlic (optional)
1 teaspoon salt

2 teaspoons cornstarch
1 tablespoon butter

Baby limas can be substituted for butter beans, if you prefer. Cook them the same way.

Put all ingredients except cornstarch and butter into saucepan; cook until beans are tender, about 10 minutes. Remove onion and garlic. Drain beans; reserve liquid.

Slightly thicken liquid with cornstarch. Add butter. Mix well; pour over beans.

Serve at once.

Yield: 4 to 6 servings.

Stir-Fried Bean Sprouts

1 tablespoon vegetable oil

2 cups bean sprouts

1 tablespoon soy sauce

Heat oil in wok or skillet. Stir-fry sprouts 1 to 2 minutes or until heated through but still crisp.

Serve at once, sprinkled with a little soy sauce.

Yield: 4 servings.

Wheat and Ginger Broccoli

¼ cup butter or margarine
1 clove garlic, minced
½ teaspoon salt
½ teaspoon ground ginger
2 tablespoons wheat germ
3 cups fresh broccoli, cut
   into bite-size pieces,
   cooked until tender-crisp

Melt butter in frying pan.
Sauté garlic until tender.
Add salt, ginger, and wheat germ. Stir-fry quickly until well
   mixed and wheat germ is just browned; be careful not
   to burn mixture.
Add broccoli; stir to coat. Heat through.

Yield: 4 to 6 servings.

Cabbage–Tomato Casserole

Preheat oven to 375°F.

½ cup chopped onions
4 tablespoons butter
3 tablespoons flour
2 cups canned tomatoes
2 tablespoons Worcester-
   shire sauce
¾ teaspoon salt
¼ teaspoon pepper
½ teaspoon sugar
6 cups finely shredded
   cabbage
3 slices bread, cubed

Sauté onions in butter until tender.

Blend in flour; stir until smooth.
Add tomatoes, Worcestershire sauce, salt, pepper, and
   sugar.

Cook cabbage in salted water 5 minutes.
Brown bread cubes in 1 tablespoon butter.

Mix drained cabbage, tomato mixture, bread, and cheese in
   2-quart casserole. Bake 30 minutes.

Yield: 4 to 6 servings.

Sesame Carrots

3 tablespoons sesame seeds
2½ tablespoons vegetable
   oil
4 cups grated carrots
Salt to taste

Sauté sesame seeds in oil until brown.

Add carrots; stir-fry quickly 1 to 2 minutes.
Salt and serve.

Yield: 5 to 6 servings.

Sweet-and-Sour Celery and Onions

1 bunch fresh celery	Trim celery; cut ribs or stalks into 1-inch pieces.
6 slices bacon	Fry bacon in large skillet until crisp. Remove bacon; drain on paper towels. Drain all but 3 tablespoons bacon drippings from skillet.
1 cup sliced onion rings	Add celery and onion rings. Sauté 5 minutes, stirring occasionally. Reduce heat; cook, covered, 12 to 15 minutes or until vegetables are crisp-tender.
3 tablespoons cider vinegar **1 tablespoon sugar** **¼ teaspoon salt** **¼ teaspoon white pepper**	Stir in vinegar, sugar, salt, and white pepper; heat through.

Spoon into serving dish; crumble bacon over top.

Yield: 6 servings.

Confetti Corn

6 ears of corn	Remove husks and silks from corn. Cook corn in boiling water 8 to 10 minutes or until tender; drain. Cool until easily handled; cut kernels from cobs.
¼ cup butter **¼ cup chopped green sweet pepper** **¼ cup chopped red sweet pepper** **1 tablespoon finely chopped fresh parsley**	Melt butter in saucepan. Add peppers and parsley. Cook over low heat, stirring constantly, until peppers are tender. Stir in corn; heat through.

Yield: 6 servings.

Corn Pudding

Preheat oven to 375°F.

1 tablespoon butter or margarine **1 tablespoon flour**	Grease 1-quart casserole. Melt butter; blend in flour.
1 cup milk, scalded **1 teaspoon salt** **⅛ teaspoon pepper** **1 teaspoon sugar**	Add milk, salt, pepper, and sugar.
1 16-ounce can cream-style corn	Add corn; heat slightly.
4 eggs, slightly beaten	Blend eggs into warm milk mixture. Pour into casserole. Place casserole in pan of hot water. Bake 1 hour or until set.

Yield: 6 servings

Vegetable Jambalaya

2 tablespoons oil
6 to 8 small mushrooms

1 cup cooked rice
1 green pepper, seeded and
    chopped
1 small onion, peeled and
    chopped
1 stalk celery, chopped
1 canned pimiento, chopped
½ cup canned or stewed
    tomatoes
Cayenne pepper
¼ teaspoon paprika
¼ cup melted butter or
    margarine
Watercress or parsley for
    garnish

Pre-heat oven to 300°.
Heat oil in pan, add mushrooms; sauté a few minutes. (If
    small mushrooms are used, leave them whole; if larger
    ones, cut into halves or quarters.)
Combine rice, mushrooms, green pepper, onion, celery,
    pimiento and tomatoes.

Add salt to taste, a few grains of cayenne pepper and
    paprika.
Add melted butter, mix well.

Put into greased casserole, cover tightly; cook about 1
    hour. Serve garnished with a small bunch of watercress
    or parsley.

Yield: 4 servings.

Potato Pancakes

2 large potatoes (grated on
    medium grater, makes
    about 2½ cups)
3 cups water
1 teaspoon lemon juice
1 boiled potato, mashed
1 egg, beaten
2 tablespoons milk
½ teaspoon salt

6 to 8 tablespoons vegetable
    oil

Grate raw potatoes into water with lemon juice. Place
    potatoes in strainer or cheesecloth; drain off liquid well.

Beat raw and cooked potatoes with egg, milk, and salt to
    form batter.

Using 3 tablespoons oil for each batch, drop batter for 3 or
    4 pancakes at a time into hot oil in large frypan. When
    firm on bottom side, loosen edges; turn. Brown other
    side.
Remove; drain on paper towels. Keep warm.
Continue until all batter is used.
Serve immediately.

Yield: 3 or 4 servings.

DESSERTS

Butterscotch Bread Pudding

Preheat oven to 350°F.

3 tablespoons margarine
½ cup brown sugar

Melt margarine in pan; add sugar.
Heat until well blended.

¼ teaspoon baking soda
2 cups milk

Dissolve baking soda in milk; add gradually to sugar mixture, stirring until well blended. Set aside to cool.

2 eggs
Pinch of salt

Beat eggs lightly.
Add salt and cooled milk-and-sugar mixture.

2 cups stale bread cubes
(about ½-inch cubes)

Put bread cubes into greased baking dish; pour custard over.

Bake about 45 minutes.

Yield: 6 servings.

Butterscotch Bread Pudding

Apple Pudding

5 to 6 good-sized cooking
   apples, peeled, cored,
   sliced
¾ cup sugar
½ teaspoon ground
   cinnamon
½ teaspoon ground nutmeg
4 tablespoons margarine
4 tablespoons hot water

1 egg

1 cup all-purpose flour
1 teaspoon baking powder
Pinch of salt

Preheat oven to 375°F.
Put apples into baking dish.

Sprinkle with ¼ cup sugar and spices; dot with 2 tablespoons margarine. Add ½ cup hot water.

Beat egg and ½ cup sugar together until thick.
Stir in 2 tablespoons melted margarine.

Sift flour, baking powder, and salt together; fold into egg mixture.
Spread on top of apple.

Bake 25 minutes.
Reduce heat to 350°F.
Bake 10 to 15 minutes.

Yield: 5 or 6 servings.

Apple Pudding

Peanut-Butter Layer Cake

Preheat oven to 350°F.
Grease and flour 2 layer cake pans 8 or 9 × 1½ inches.

2 eggs
½ cup granulated sugar

Separate eggs; beat whites until fluffy. Add granulated sugar; continue beating until stiff and glossy.

2¼ cups cake flour
3 teaspoons baking powder
1 teaspoon salt
¼ teaspoon baking soda
1 cup brown sugar, well packed
⅓ cup peanut butter
⅓ cup vegetable oil
1¼ cups milk

Sift flour, baking powder, salt, and baking soda together into bowl.

Add brown sugar, ⅓ cup peanut butter, oil, and ½ the milk; beat well.
Add remaining milk and egg yolks; beat again. (If using mixer, beat 1 minute each time at medium speed.)
Fold in egg-white mixture lightly.
Put into prepared pans.

Bake 30 to 35 minutes.
Leave in pans to cool a little.
Turn out on rack.

Peanut-Butter Frosting

¼ cup peanut butter
3 cups sifted confectioners' sugar
4 to 5 tablespoons milk

Blend ¼ cup peanut butter with sugar; add enough milk to make creamy consistency.
Use it to sandwich layers together; spread rest over top.

If desired, decorate top with peanuts.

Yield: 8- or 9-inch 2-layer cake.

Peanut-Butter Layer Cake

Coffee Dessert

Coffee Dessert

1½ envelopes unflavored
    gelatin
1½ cups water
1 cup milk
¾ cup sugar
¼ teaspoon salt
2 tablespoons instant coffee
    powder
3 eggs (separated)

1 teaspoon vanilla extract

Put gelatin, water, milk, sugar, salt, and coffee in double boiler. Heat, stirring, until gelatin has melted and mixture just reaches boiling point.

Add egg yolks; stir over low heat until mixture is thick enough to coat back of spoon.

Remove from heat; add vanilla.
Chill until mixture thickens to a syrupy consistency.
Beat egg whites until stiff; fold into mixture.
Pour into sherbet glasses; chill until firm.
Decorate as desired.

Yield: 6 servings.

INDEX

64